O9-BUA-479

The GREAT MOLASSES FLOOD

Boston, 1919

The GREAT MOLASSES FLOOD

Boston, 1919

Deborah Kops

ini Charlesbridge

For John, Noah, Cecile, Grant, Deborah, Ben, and Jonah, with love

Text copyright © 2012 by Deborah Kops
Map on page x copyright © 2012 by Sarah Brannen
All rights reserved, including the right of reproduction in whole or in part in any form.
Charlesbridge and colophon are registered trademarks of Charlesbridge Publishing, Inc.

Published by Charlesbridge
85 Main Street
Watertown, MA 02472
(617) 926-0329
www.charlesbridge.com

Library of Congress Cataloging-in-Publication Data
Kops, Deborah.
    The Great Molasses Flood : Boston, 1919 / Deborah Kops.
        p. cm.
    ISBN 978-1-58089-348-0 (reinforced for library use)
1. Industrial accidents—Massachusetts—Boston—History—
20th century—Juvenile literature. 2. Molasses industry—
Accidents—Massachusetts—Boston—History—20th century—
Juvenile literature. 3. Alcohol industry—Accidents—Massachusetts—
Boston—History—20th century—Juvenile literature. 4. Floods—
Massachusetts—Boston—History—20th century—Juvenile literature.
5. Boston (Mass.)—History—Juvenile literature. I. Title.
HD7262.5.U62M334 2011
363.17—dc22   2011000655

Printed in China
(hc) 10 9 8 7 6 5 4 3 2 1

Display type and text type set in Goudy Sans and Stempel Garamond
Color separations by Jade Productions
Printed and bound September 2011 by Jade Productions in Heyuan, Guangdong, China
Production supervision by Brian G. Walker
Designed by Diane M. Earley

Contents

Cast of Characters

John Barry worked in the North End Paving Yard.

Samuel Blair hauled gravel and stone for the North End Paving Division to work sites around the city.

Wilfred Bolster was the chief justice of Boston's Municipal Court.

Charles Choate was a lawyer who represented the U.S. Industrial Alcohol Company (USIA) during the molasses trial.

Martin Clougherty owned the Pen and Pencil bar and lived across Commercial Street from the molasses tank.

Teresa Clougherty lived with her brothers, Martin and Stephen Clougherty, and her mother, Bridget Clougherty.

John Dillon worked in the train yard as a train car inspector.

Antonio DiStasio was a nine-year-old boy who lived near the molasses tank.

Maria DiStasio was Antonio's eleven-year-old sister.

John Flynn worked in the train yard fixing broken tubs and barrels used for shipping.

William Gillespie was a fireman who worked in the Engine 31 firehouse.

Isaac Gonzales once worked at the molasses tank doing odd jobs, but had quit before the flood.

Damon Hall was a lawyer who represented the people and businesses who were suing USIA.

Pasquale and **Vincenzo Iantosca** were brothers who lived downstairs from their friends Antonio and Maria DiStasio.

Arthur Jell was the assistant treasurer of USIA. He was in charge of the molasses tank on Commercial Street.

George Kakavas sold bananas from a small cart in the North End.

Stavroula Kakavas was the daughter of George Kakavas.

John Lawton supervised the children's playground and the beach in North End Park.

George Layhe was a fireman with Engine Company 31.

Frank McManus was a policeman who patrolled the neighborhood surrounding the molasses tank.

Walter Merrithew worked as a freight clerk in the train yard near the molasses tank.

Elizabeth O'Brien was an elderly woman who lived with her sister in an apartment east of the molasses tank.

Hugh Ogden was a lawyer who acted as a judge during the molasses trial.

Walter Wedger was an expert on explosives who worked for the Massachusetts State Police.

Prologue

Of all the disasters that have occurred in the United States, the Great Molasses Flood in Boston was one of the most bizarre. Imagine a city neighborhood awash in molasses: that dark brown, sweet-and-sour liquid that sticks to everything like honey—the same stuff that makes gingerbread men taste so good.

It sounds like a bad joke. But as the people of Boston discovered on January 15, 1919, a dark, rushing wave of molasses can be as destructive as a tornado.

The people who lived along the narrow, hilly streets of Boston's North End and worked on the nearby waterfront were not expecting a disaster. In fact, they thought life in Boston was getting better.

The city's battle with a terrible disease had just ended. In late August 1918 a mysterious illness called the Spanish influenza had arrived on the shores of the United States. Boston was the first stop on its deadly race through the country.

In early October the mayor of Boston closed the city's schools, churches, and dance halls to try to keep the disease from spreading. A month later the worst of the epidemic was over in the city. Six thousand Boston residents had died of the flu.

By late fall 1918 things in Boston were looking up. Everyone had been thrilled when Babe Ruth helped the Red Sox win the World Series. Then in November the fighting in Europe stopped. The Great War was finally over, and the American troops—hundreds of thousands of them—were coming home.

January 1919 was a hopeful time. Schools had reopened. So had the soda fountains, where kids went to buy Cokes. On New Year's Eve tens of thousands of cheering, singing Bostonians gathered to ring in the new year. They jammed the city's cafés and hotels and overflowed into the streets. Everyone seemed thrilled that life in this old port city was returning to normal.

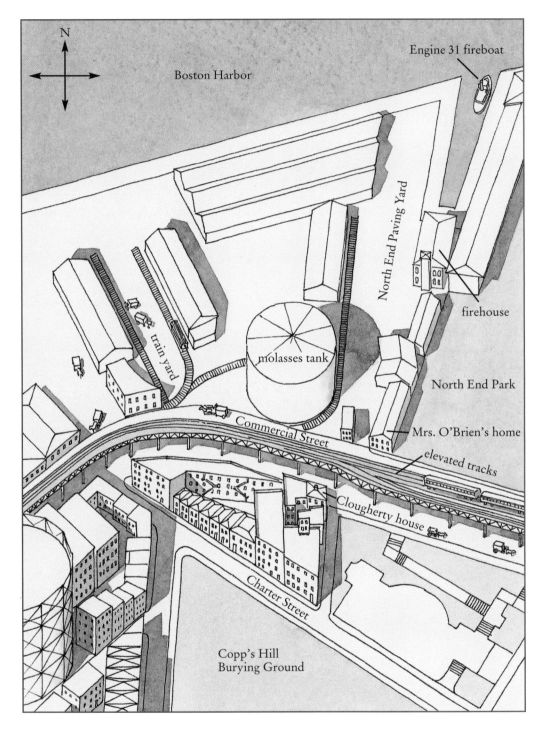

Boston's North End, vicinity of the molasses tank

Chapter 1

Lunchtime Near the Harbor

January 15 was a sunny day. By lunchtime the temperature had reached forty-three degrees Fahrenheit. That was downright toasty for a winter afternoon in Boston, Massachusetts.

In the city's North End, close to the harbor, Martin Clougherty was still asleep. He had been up until four o'clock in the morning working at the bar he owned, the Pen and Pencil. With a name like that, it was no wonder the bar was popular with newspaper reporters.

Martin had not yet seen the big headline in the *Boston Post*. "Seven More States Join 'Dry Column'," the newspaper shrieked—referring to states that had just ratified the Eighteenth Amendment to the Constitution. If the amendment became law, it would be illegal for Martin or anyone else to sell or consume alcoholic drinks. He would have to close the Pen and Pencil.

Now it was time to get up. Martin, who was thirty-seven years old, lived with his mother; his sister, Teresa; and his brother, Stephen. Teresa woke him. Their mother had just put lunch on the table for them and their boarders, the two men who paid to eat and sleep in their home.

The wooden building where the Cloughertys lived overlooked Commercial Street, one of the busiest roads in Boston. Trucks and cars whizzed by the horse-drawn wagons. Many of them were Ford Model T cars and Model TT trucks. But plenty of wagons still came clip-clopping down the road. Above the street, on the elevated train tracks, passenger trains rumbled by as they traveled between the city's two big railway stations—North Station and South Station.

Whenever the Cloughertys looked out the kitchen window, they couldn't help noticing another big structure, beyond the elevated tracks. An ugly steel tank about fifty feet high loomed over the old houses and commercial buildings of this seaside neighborhood. The tank held molasses, and on January 15, it was very full.

Just a few days earlier, the *Mielero* had steamed into Boston's inner harbor from the Caribbean Sea with a load of molasses. The tanker tied up at a wharf on the nearby waterfront. Men pumped

North Market Street, Boston

the molasses in the tanker through a pipeline, which ran from the wharf to the molasses tank. When they finished, the tank on Commercial Street held 2,319,525 gallons of molasses.

The molasses was heavy. It weighed about 13,000 tons (26,000,000 pounds)—around the same weight as 13,000 Ford cars.

At about 12:30 on this sunny day in January, many of the people who lived or worked near the molasses tank were relaxing over lunch. Others were busy.

MOLASSES INTO RUM

Men pumped molasses from the big storage tank near Commercial Street into barrels. The barrels were loaded into freight cars at the train yard right near the tank, and from there freight trains regularly brought the molasses over to a factory in Cambridge, just a few miles away. There it was made into alcohol, which was in turn used to make ammunition. Thank goodness the army no longer needed a lot of ammunition: World War I had ended on November 11, and the soldiers were coming home. The company that owned the tank, the U.S. Industrial Alcohol Company (USIA), found another use for the molasses. It would soon be made into rum, an alcoholic drink.

New England merchants had been receiving molasses from Caribbean islands and making it into rum for about two centuries. Molasses came from sugar cane plants, which grew on these warm, tropical islands. When island workers boiled the juice from the plants, they got two products: sugar crystals and molasses.

USIA was in a hurry to start making a type of alcohol from molasses that distillers could turn into rum. There was a reason for the big rush: Congress had recently approved the Eighteenth Amendment to the U.S. Constitution, which would make it illegal to sell or drink alcoholic beverages. The amendment became known as the Prohibition Amendment, because alcoholic drinks would be prohibited. Many Americans believed that drinking alcohol got too many men and their families into trouble. They thought it led to unemployment, violence, and poverty.

By the end of the day on January 15, thirty-five states had ratified the Eighteenth Amendment. When the thirty-sixth state voted yes, it would become part of the Constitution. A year after the amendment was ratified, laws banning drinking would go into effect. That's why USIA was in a hurry. It only had about one year to make alcohol for rum.

IN THE TRAIN YARD

John Dillon, a train car inspector, was moving some freight cars around in the train yard next to the molasses tank. Nearby, some men were unloading their horse-drawn wagons. The horses were big and broad, with hooves the size of dinner plates. One truck man with a load of glass bottles backed up his two horses to Number 2 freight house. Another pulled up to Number 4 with twenty barrels of sugar. Walter Merrithew, a freight clerk, was helping a truck man find the goods he had come to pick up at Number 3 freight house, the shed closest to the water.

While these men worked in the yard, others were still eating lunch. John Flynn, a cooper, had just gotten a shave at a local barbershop. Flynn's job was to repair broken tubs and barrels used for shipping. Now he headed for the small room in Number 3 where he and his friends liked to eat.

Four people in the train yard did not work there. They were much too young. Antonio DiStasio, who was nine years old, liked

The molasses tank

to taste the molasses that leaked from the tank. So did his sister Maria, who was eleven, and the two brothers who lived downstairs from them, Pasquale and Vincenzo Iantosca. Like other neighborhood children they scraped molasses off the side of the tank with sticks and licked it off. Candy made from molasses, like Cracker Jack or caramels, tasted better, but the molasses leaking out of the tank was free. Antonio, Maria, and their friends often gathered around the tank like bees.

The children also gathered scrap wood lying around, which their parents burned to heat their homes. Wood was in short supply now, and New England winters were long and cold.

While John Dillon was shifting the train cars that afternoon, he saw Maria gathering wood. She and the boys were near a loading platform for freight trains. A supervisor who worked in the train yard saw Maria, too, and went over to scold her. A train yard was not a safe place for children.

WASH DAY AT MRS. O'BRIEN'S

Just beyond the train yard to the east, Elizabeth O'Brien was taking advantage of the good weather. She was washing her clothes in a washtub at the back of her apartment, which she shared with her grown son and her sister. Then she was going to hang the wash outside to dry on a clothesline. The sisters, who lived on the same side of Commercial Street as the molasses tank, had already eaten their lunch.

Mrs. O'Brien's apartment was on the second floor of a building that belonged to the City of Boston's North End Paving Division. Below was a blacksmith shop and some offices, where Mrs. O'Brien went when she needed to make a phone call. Before she began her wash, she had called someone about a big tag sale in Boston the previous Saturday. Six hundred women had spread out all over the city to raise money for men in the Twenty-sixth Infantry Division of the U.S. Army, which was still in Europe. Mrs. O'Brien was helping with this volunteer effort. After all, the Twenty-sixth was New England's own "Yankee Division," which included many young men from Boston. Her own husband, who was no longer living, had fought in the Civil War.

The North End Paving Yard was right behind Mrs. O'Brien's apartment. During most of the day, the air rang with the sounds of stonecutters drilling and splitting granite rocks for the city's sidewalks and train platforms. But at 12:30 the yard was quiet.

Samuel Blair worked in the paving yard. He had already hauled two loads of gravel and stone on his one-horse dump cart to a work site in the city. Now he was having his lunch in a carriage shed with six other workers in one of the buildings. Nearby, the city's horses ate in their stalls, rustling and crunching their hay.

BOSTON'S OLDEST NEIGHBORHOOD

The molasses tank stood on the edge of the North End, Boston's oldest neighborhood. In 1919 a number of buildings in the North End dated from the time of the American Revolution. The house that Paul Revere once lived in was still standing on North Square, uphill from the molasses tank on Commercial Street. In fact, the small house, with its windows made from little diamond-shaped panes of glass, was already about one hundred years old when Revere lived there.

The Old North Church was still standing, too. On April 18, 1775, Paul Revere asked a member of the church to shine two lanterns in the bell tower. They were a signal that the British were crossing the harbor by boat before heading inland toward the towns of Lexington and Concord.

Two months later, on June 17, 1775, Redcoats fired a cannon from Copp's Hill Burying Ground, in the North End. The British were aiming at the Patriots across the water in the town of Charlestown, where the Battle of Bunker Hill was raging.

The burial ground was still there in 1919. It was the highest point in the neighborhood. A family out for a walk could stand at one end of the cemetery and look out at Boston's busy inner harbor. They would certainly notice the molasses tank on Commercial Street looming over the neighborhood. Beyond the tank, at the inner harbor, the Charles River and the Mystic River flowed into the Atlantic Ocean. And across the water they could see the hills of Charlestown.

AT THE FIREHOUSE

Over at the wooden firehouse, beyond the paving yard, four fire-men were playing a card game called whist. Their engine, Number 31, did not roll out of the firehouse with a blaring siren like most fire engines in Boston. Engine 31 was docked on the water right outside. It was a fireboat. When there was a fire on one of the many wharves jutting out into the water, the men motored over in Engine 31 and sprayed streams of ocean water at the fire, right from the coal-powered boat.

When there was no emergency, the firehouse was a friendly place. John Barry, a stonecutter who worked in the paving yard, liked to come over at lunchtime and talk with the guys. Now he was filling his pipe with tobacco and watching the card game. George Layhe, a fireman, announced that he was taking a short nap and began heading for the third floor, where the beds were. William Gillespie was already up there. He wanted something from his locker, which was near the sleeping room.

NORTH END PARK

Meanwhile, inside North End Park, east of the fireboat, John Law-ton was sitting in his office. Lawton worked for Boston's recreation department. He supervised the park's playground for children and, in the summer, the swimming beach. When he looked out his window, he could see the molasses tank to the west. But Lawton was not interested in gazing at the ugly tank. It was time for him to leave the office and get some lunch.

Not far away, Patrolman Frank McManus was getting ready to call in at the police signal box on Commercial Street. As usual, the lunch hour was pretty quiet on his waterfront beat. But even when things seemed peaceful, trouble might be brewing. Members of a violent political organization called the American Anarchists had just tacked disturbing posters on a few of the city's telephone poles. The group threatened to bomb the city, but they didn't say where. "We will dynamite you!" they warned.

Patrolman McManus knew that local anarchists and other violent groups did a lot more than make threats. Two years earlier some men had planted a bomb outside a police station on Salutation Street, near the harbor. The bomb blew a three-foot hole in a wall. People felt the shock of the explosion all over the harborside neighborhood. And it left residents all over Boston feeling uneasy.

Chapter 2

A Terrible Wave

Martin Clougherty, the owner of the Pen and Pencil, was in his bed rubbing the sleep from his eyes. His sister, Teresa, had just awakened him and was still in his bedroom. Suddenly, she let out a scream. "Something terrible has happened to the molasses tank!" she cried. Martin shoved the curtains aside and saw a murky liquid swirling outside. He gave his sister a hug and said, "Stay here." Before he could investigate the situation, he heard his mother shriek in the kitchen. A moment later Martin went sailing through the air.

A wave of molasses had lifted the Cloughertys' house right off its foundation and pushed it across Commercial Street toward the elevated train. The house smashed against the columns supporting the tracks. The next thing Martin Clougherty knew, he was in a dark sea surrounded by pieces of his house, and he could not stand up. He was facing the ocean. Had he fallen in? he wondered. Clougherty managed to get his nose out of the goo and took some deep breaths. Something was floating on the surface, something he could use for a raft. He tried to swim toward it, but the dark sea was too thick, and he couldn't move. Luckily a wave pushed the raft right in his direction. It was a bed, and Clougherty, who was still in his pajamas, climbed on top.

He looked around. His neighborhood had suddenly become a strange world. Sticking up out of the heavy liquid was a limp hand. Could it be his sister? As he pulled the body up onto the raft, he saw that it really was Teresa. And thank goodness, she was alive.

THE VIEW FROM ABOVE

At about 12:40 the brakeman on the elevated line was standing near the window of a passenger train, which had left South Station about five minutes earlier. As the train neared the molasses tank, the brakeman heard a loud noise, like metal ripping apart. He looked down to see the molasses tank split wide open and a wave of molasses heading toward the tracks.

As the train came around a curve, there was another surprise. The molasses hurled a great chunk of the tank against two columns supporting the elevated tracks. A moment later one of the El supports bent as if it was just a skinny twig. Part of the El's tracks, which the train had passed over just seconds before, sagged toward the road below.

The brakeman didn't waste any time. He pulled the emergency bell to signal the motorman. Then he pulled the brake to stop the train and jumped off. Another train would be coming from South Station soon. If it didn't stop in time, it would tumble right off the elevated tracks onto the pavement below. The brakeman made his way past the sagging track and soon spotted the oncoming train. He signaled frantically, and to his great relief, the train stopped. The motorman on the oncoming train saw the broken track ahead of him. He raced through four cars, put the train in reverse, and began chugging toward South Station, avoiding a terrible train wreck.

Below, on Commercial Street, Patrolman Frank McManus had watched in amazement as the top of the tank floated right off and the wave of molasses began rushing toward the elevated tracks. A second wave came right at him, and he ran uphill, barely staying ahead of the dark, sticky tide, which soon coated his uniform.

AT THE TRAIN YARD

Antonio DiStasio was still in the train yard with his sister Maria and their friends when the molasses tank gave an ear-splitting

The elevated tracks twisted into new shapes after the molasses disaster

rumble and ripped open. A sea of molasses quickly surrounded them. Antonio ran for his life, but he was no match for the tide. It dragged him along, shoving him into a curb. Ouch! The curb knocked out two of his teeth. Then a piece of steel from the tank, which was floating in the current, hit him and cut his head. The molasses pushed him farther and farther away from home, toward the harbor. Where was Maria? Who would save him? Antonio had never been so frightened in his life.

John Flynn, the cooper, had just stepped onto the platform of Number 3 freight house when he heard the molasses tank, about one hundred feet away, bursting apart. He turned around to see what the noise was. Suddenly everything seemed to be moving toward him—automobiles, horses and wagons, and train cars.

A truck hurled through the freight shed ahead of Flynn and pushed open the doors at the back. Flynn sailed through the doors and felt the ice-cold water of the Charles River on his back. He had landed in the harbor. One of his legs soon became tangled in a bale of scrap and dragged him under the water. Grabbing hold of a floating oil barrel, Flynn pulled himself to the surface. He managed to untangle his leg and swam around the wreckage, looking for a safe place to rest. A big bale of cotton floated nearby. "Get up on the bale! Get up on the bale!" someone shouted. Flynn looked up. It was one of his lunch buddies. Four of them had climbed onto the roof of Number 3 freight house to escape the molasses. Flynn wished he was on that roof. He tried to pull himself on top of the bale, but it was too big. How long could he possibly survive in the water in the middle of the winter?

Meanwhile the moving mass of molasses and freight had trapped shipping clerk Walter Merrithew inside the freight house. The freight, including a bag of leather scraps, was pushing him toward the open doors that Flynn had gone through just moments before. Merrithew's feet were not even touching the floor, and he could not find a way to fight the rushing tide. He was helpless.

The car inspector John Dillon was luckier. He had been moving a freight car when he heard the molasses tank burst open. When the molasses reached him, it dragged the train car only a few feet. But a horse drowned in the molasses right near the train car. Dillon glanced around the neighborhood. It looked as if it had been hit by a hurricane—but the "rain" was like soft tar. Near the sagging tracks of the elevated line, the wet electric wires sputtered and flashed. In the distance, a player piano floated silently on the sea of sticky goop.

MRS. O'BRIEN LOSES MORE THAN HER WASH

Mrs. O'Brien was doing her wash in a back room of the building in which she and her sister lived. At 12:40 she was still at her washtub when she heard a loud noise. A heavy team of horses must have backed up and hit the building, she thought—and then she lost consciousness. When she came to, she was soaking wet and lying underneath the washtub, which had fallen on her.

Mrs. O'Brien stood up and opened the door that connected the back room to the rest of the apartment. Her sister would certainly be amazed at this bizarre accident and would surely give Mrs. O'Brien a bit of sympathy, which Mrs. O'Brien needed right then. But her sister wasn't there—and neither was the rest of their apartment. The front of the building had completely collapsed. What happened to her sister? And what on earth could have destroyed their home? Mrs. O'Brien didn't know what to do. Although she did not yet realize it, a wave of molasses had moved her building all the way to North End Park.

On the way to the park, that same terrible wave picked up a few buildings in the North End Paving Yard. One of them was the carriage shed, where Samuel Blair had been eating his lunch with six other men. A few minutes later he was on the beach, lying in a mix of molasses and water, about ten feet from dry land. Blair looked around. There was no sign of the carriage shed or of his friends. He tried to get up. No luck. Blair noticed the USS *Nantucket* tied up at a nearby wharf, and he shouted for help as loudly as he could.

AT THE FIREHOUSE

The men playing cards at the firehouse looked out the windows and saw a dark wall that didn't belong there. Whatever it was, the wall was coming right at them. "Oh, my God!" one of them cried.

Two of the card players ran to the double doors leading to the dock, where the fireboat sat peacefully on the water. If they jumped into the water, they could try to escape the rushing wave. But the building suddenly turned dark as the molasses hit it and covered the windows. The men never reached the door. The ceiling came crashing down, and with it an assortment of wooden beams and heating pipes.

Most of the men had no way to escape. A pipe pinned one fireman down, while a wooden beam trapped another. A third man landed near the fireman's pole, with a piece of heavy wood and a steam pipe pinning him down in a painful position. John Barry, the stonecutter who had been watching the card game, lay under a beam and a water heater. George Layhe, who had been on his way to the third floor to take a nap, was in the most hopeless position of all: a big piece of wood lay on top of him, and over the wood was a heavy pool table and a piano.

William Gillespie was one of the few men in the building who could still move. He was already on the third floor when the wave reached the building. His head hit a corner of the ceiling and he was knocked completely off his feet. When Gillespie got up, he felt dazed.

Was he dizzy, or was the building really rocking? Every time he took a step, the building seemed to move. He was being pushed toward the sleeping room, where the beds were moving around as if they were caught in a whirlpool. Gillespie braced himself against a wall, afraid of falling out a window. He managed to avoid the whirling beds and headed downstairs.

Then Gillespie saw the wreckage. The second story had collapsed on top of the first. He heard voices. "Get me out," someone groaned. Another voice moaned, "My God, I am dying." "For God's sake, try and get me out!" a third man yelled.

Gillespie quickly found four of the men who were trapped. He managed to move the heavy piece of wood that lay across the man near the pole so he could straighten out his body a bit. But Gillespie had to be careful not to step on another man's head. He wanted to free the men, but there was molasses everywhere. And there was no equipment around to help him move the heavy pipes and beams. He needed to find some more able-bodied men—fast. Gillespie looked for an open exit, but the doors were blocked. He saw a window and jumped. Was he flying? It felt like it. He was getting dizzier by the minute. Gillespie had hit his head pretty hard when he was on the third floor. And the building was still rocking. Although he didn't realize it, a section of the molasses tank had knocked the firehouse right off its foundation.

The Engine 31 firehouse after the disaster

IN NORTH END PARK

A few minutes after the molasses tank burst open, John Lawton, the supervisor at North End Park, saw a big, black mass rushing toward the park. He instantly recognized most of the structures sitting on top. They were small buildings that belonged to the North End Paving Yard, and they seemed to be rising on this tide and heading in Lawton's direction. But suddenly, the moving wall of molasses sank to the ground right outside his window and spread out toward the beach. The buildings that had been riding on the molasses came crashing down and fell apart.

Lawton ran out of his building and pulled a police alarm. For a moment, before the rescuers arrived, a hush fell over the area. It may only have been for a few seconds, just long enough for people to look around and try to understand what had happened to this small neighborhood by the harbor.

Chapter 3

Hundreds to the Rescue

About a dozen ambulances from the Red Cross organization arrived at the scene of the disaster. All of them were driven by women filling in for the men who had left their jobs to fight in the Great War. Other ambulances soon arrived from the city's police department, local hospitals, the U.S. Army, and the U.S. Navy. For at least an hour, the drivers clanged their bells as they sped through the streets.

Hundreds of rescue workers blanketed the neighborhood. One hundred sixteen sailors from the USS *Nantucket* rushed across the North End Pier to help. More sailors arrived from the USS *Bessie J*.

WOMEN WANT TO VOTE

When the United States entered the Great War in 1917, life changed for a lot of women. After millions of men left for the battlegrounds of Europe, there were many important jobs that had to be filled. Women who needed to support their families while the men were away stepped up to do those jobs. They drove ambulances, delivered mail, operated streetcars, and worked in factories. Some manufactured ammunition. About one million women went to work for the first time. Wealthier women often did volunteer work. For example, they found ways to raise money for food and equipment for American soldiers.

These women were helping to keep the country going, and they were supporting American soldiers. In return, many of them demanded a basic right that they did not have: they could not vote. White men had been helping to shape the nation's history with their ballots since the founding of the United States in 1776. African American men had finally been given the right to vote when the states ratified the Fifteenth Amendment to the Constitution in 1870, after the Civil War. An amendment giving women the right to vote was not ready for ratification. Congress had to approve it first. But it had been voting the amendment down every year since it was proposed in 1878. At the time of the molasses flood in 1919, women were hoping Congress would finally change its mind. Woodrow Wilson, the president of the United States, had decided to support the amendment. He was urging Congress to pass it.

They waded into the molasses and looked for survivors among the wrecked buildings. Within a few minutes their blue uniforms and even their skin had turned a shade of copper. Molasses covered them from head to foot.

The sailors were joined by policemen. Firemen made sure there were no fires to put out. Then they pitched in, too, searching for people trapped in the ruins of the collapsed buildings.

Early on the rescuers found the body of Maria DiStasio. She had become trapped in a pile of molasses barrels. The rescuers did not know her name. They sadly placed her on a stretcher, and an ambulance took her to the morgue, where the bodies of the dead were kept until they could be identified.

Some of the rescuers worked through the night. When the Red Cross drivers saw that their ambulances were no longer needed, they found another way to help. The women handed workers coffee, donuts, and other food.

While rescuers searched for survivors, relatives waited anxiously across Commercial Street. They worried about husbands, wives, sons, and daughters who might have been injured—or maybe even killed. Occasionally someone cried out in terror or grief.

City officials began arriving. Boston's new mayor, Andrew Peters, came. So did John F. Fitzgerald, a popular ex-mayor. The sight of the fallen elevated tracks, collapsed buildings, crushed automobiles, and dead horses shocked the officials. The mayor promised there would be an investigation to find out what had caused the disaster.

No one seemed to notice any representatives of USIA, which owned the molasses tank. Arthur Jell, a senior official in charge of the tank, was probably sitting in his office in Cambridge, just a few miles west of Boston.

In addition to the rescuers and city officials, crowds of people gathered near the disaster site. Word of the disaster had spread quickly, and everyone wanted to see the neighborhood flooded with molasses. More police arrived to keep the crowds from getting in the way of the rescuers.

When the sightseers left, they took souvenirs of the disaster with them. The molasses coated their shoes, and they spread a trail of sticky brown goo all over the city—in streetcars, on sidewalks, and in office buildings.

MARTIN CLOUGHERTY SEARCHES FOR HIS MOTHER

Someone helped Martin Clougherty bring his sister, Teresa, to a neighbor's house. Teresa, who was dazed, mumbled the word "Mother." Where was their mother? Martin realized that he did not know whether Mrs. Clougherty was alive. He left Teresa with the neighbor and called loudly for Mrs. Clougherty over and over for what seemed like an hour. Eventually someone gave him the sad news. Rescue workers had found her, but she was dead. Martin's brother, Stephen, was alive, though. Some sailors had rescued him and taken him to the Haymarket Relief Station, a small hospital south of the neighborhood.

THE DiStasios' Story

Nine-year-old Antonio DiStasio wished he could call out to his mother. As the molasses pushed him toward the harbor, he heard her shouting his name. He could not answer because he had swallowed molasses and was choking. But he could still use his arms. When a fireman extended a pole toward him, Antonio grabbed it, and the fireman pulled him out of the rushing tide.

Antonio's adventures were not over, though. An ambulance sped him to the Haymarket Relief Station. While he was still on a stretcher, he lost consciousness. Hospital workers assumed that he had died and covered him with a sheet.

When Antonio regained consciousness, he pushed aside the sheet covering his face. What a surprise for the hospital workers! His parents, who had been looking for him all afternoon, were thrilled to learn he was alive. But where was his sister, Maria? The DiStasios were desperate to find out. They spent the night looking for her, not knowing that rescuers had found Maria's body many hours earlier. They received the terrible news the next day.

Pasquale Iantosca, one of Antonio and Maria's friends, had also drowned in the molasses. He was ten years old. His younger brother, Vincenzo, managed to get away from the molasses and made it back to their apartment, across Commercial Street.

At the Haymarket Relief Station, the white uniforms of the nurses helping the molasses-covered patients were soon streaked with brown. The molasses also hardened on the patients' clothing. So instead of removing a man's shirt to examine him, a nurse had to cut the shirt off.

Sometimes the medical workers couldn't tell whether the person on a stretcher was a man or a woman. At least twice, they put a man in a room with women patients. When they cleaned off the molasses, they discovered their mistake. All forty-two patient rooms in the hospital were soon filled with people injured in the flood.

SURVIVORS FROM THE TRAIN YARD

John Flynn, the cooper, took a roundabout route to the relief station. He had practically flown right through Number 3 freight house and landed in the Charles River. He waited for help, probably wondering if he would freeze to death in the water. A man piloting a small boat noticed him and fished him out. The boatman transferred Flynn to a Navy destroyer. Sailors wrapped his chilled body in warm blankets and took him to the Charlestown Navy Yard, across the river.

Eventually Flynn arrived at the Haymarket Relief Station. It was hard to breathe, and his head throbbed.

Walter Merrithew, inside Number 3 freight house, had been caught in a moving mass of molasses and freight pushing him toward the opening in the back of the shed. He had watched helplessly as other men, injured and in pain, cried for help.

A man who worked in the train yard noticed Merrithew. It was a miracle, because this worker was disabled: he could neither hear nor speak. With the help of another man, he freed Merrithew before the molasses could push Merrithew out the opening and into the harbor.

Merrithew ended up at Boston City Hospital. He left the same day on a new pair of crutches to take his weight off his bruised leg. He could have stayed in the hospital for at least one night, but he really wanted to go home.

Merrithew, who was only twenty years old, found little comfort at home. Although he usually shared a room with his brothers, his parents gave him his own room the night of January 15. But it was hard to sleep. He could not help thinking about the other men he had seen trapped in the freight house. In his dreams he was still trapped himself, and he yelled loudly for help. "I was making so much noise nobody could sleep," he said later. "As soon as I closed my eyes, I would see it all over again."

Wreckage under the elevated tracks

THE RESCUE IN THE ENGINE 31 FIREHOUSE

William Gillespie had jumped out the window of the firehouse to escape the collapsing building and get some help. When he got outside, he bumped into his boss, the lieutenant in charge of the firehouse. Gillespie quickly told him about the men trapped inside. Then Gillespie, who was feeling dizzier by the moment, got himself to the Haymarket Relief Station.

The lieutenant rushed to a corner of the building and signaled someone on the street to pull a fire alarm. Within minutes about twenty-five firemen arrived at the firehouse, which the molasses had dragged ten feet closer to the water. Axmen began cutting away some of the walls of the collapsed firehouse so they could reach the men. After four long hours of work, rescuers managed to free two trapped firemen.

The rescuers heard another man groaning. But a large piece of the molasses tank blocked them from reaching him. Two firemen ran and got an acetylene torch. They burned a hole in the metal big enough for a person to walk through. The groaning man must be George Layhe, they thought. A roll call for the Engine 31 Company had been taken, and Layhe was the only fireman left in the building.

The groaning man was not George Layhe. He was John Barry, the stonecutter. Barry was lying facedown, with a water heater and heavy planks of wood from the fallen firehouse on top of his back.

While the rescuers worked to free him, one worker gave Barry injections of painkiller to make him more comfortable. At about four o'clock the firemen finally removed Barry from the building.

But where was George Layhe? Someone remembered that he was about to take a nap when the molasses struck the firehouse. The rescuers, who were also firemen, called his name, but they heard no reply. When they finally found him, his body was still warm. But Layhe was dead. His hands and face were covered with molasses. He had been pinned, face up, under a pool table and a piano. With heavy hearts the rescuers loaded the body into an ambulance. Layhe's wife would have to identify his body at the hospital.

Just a few feet away from the ruins of the toppled firehouse for Engine 31, the fireboat sat peacefully on the water. It was unharmed, though it had turned an odd shade of brown. Days of work lay ahead to remove its coating of molasses.

CRIES FOR HELP IN THE PARK

John Lawton, the park supervisor, had seen the buildings from the North End Paving Yard ride into the park on a wave of molasses and collapse. After he pulled the police alarm, he waded into the molasses. He worked for hours among the shattered buildings to help rescue victims.

Lawton recognized several people who worked or lived in the

A rescuer cuts the molasses tank into sections with an acetylene torch to search for victims underneath.

neighborhood. He saw Mrs. Clougherty's body on its way to the morgue. Lawton recognized an elderly messenger who worked in the paving yard. That man was alive, but in terrible shape. How much longer would he live?

And there was John Barry, the stonecutter, who had been rescued from the nearby fire station. While he waited for an ambulance, Barry asked Lawton to tell his daughter he would not be home that evening. But he didn't want Lawton to say he'd been injured. His family would worry too much.

The sailors from the *Nantucket* were working in the park, along with Lawton and some firemen. Patrolman Frank McManus was there, too. After outrunning the molasses he had returned to summon help and to pitch in himself.

Suddenly the rescue workers heard faint cries coming from a smashed building. They listened carefully. These were not the cries of trapped workers from the paving yard. No—they sounded like a couple of elderly women.

Patrolman McManus climbed inside a window of the building with some sailors. Inside the collapsed part of the building they found Mrs. O'Brien's sister. Mrs. O'Brien had not been able to find her. Her sister was very much alive, though. When the men took her out, she promptly fainted, but she seemed unhurt. They quickly put her in an ambulance bound for one of the hospitals.

A fireman helped Mrs. O'Brien out of the building. The section she had been standing in, doing her wash, did not collapse. But she had taken a bad fall, and her jaw was broken. What was her building doing in the park? she wondered. There wasn't much left of it. When her adult son arrived, he took her to Boston City Hospital.

MORE SURVIVORS ALONG THE WATER

The carriage shed that once stood in the North End Paving Yard now lay in ruins in the park. Five of the six workers who had been eating their lunch in the shed with Samuel Blair were dead. Somehow, Blair was thrown from the carriage shed and landed on the beach near North End Park. He was covered with molasses. Six sailors from the *Nantucket* carried him to the bathhouse to wait for an ambulance to arrive.

At the end of the day, city officials counted eleven people who had died in the flood. But the officials knew the number would probably rise. The molasses had injured another fifty people, and a few of them might not live much longer. And there was still a possibility that workers would find more bodies in the rubble between the train yard and North End Park.

Horses died in the flood, too. Twenty horses belonging to the North End Paving Yard drowned. Others died in the train yard, but no one was sure how many.

Firemen standing in thick molasses after the disaster

Below the elevated tracks lie pools of molasses and a piece of the molasses tank.

ANARCHISTS IN BOSTON SPREAD FEAR

A small group of anarchists held secret meetings in East Boston. That neighborhood was opposite the North End, on the other side of the inner harbor. Anarchists believed that people could live more happily and peacefully if there was no government to interfere with their lives. Some anarchists were not exactly peaceful, though. They thought that in order to get rid of governments, they had to use violence. The group in East Boston shared that belief. Their inspiration was a man named Luigi Galleani, who published an anarchist newspaper. He lived in Lynn, a town north of Boston.

Galleani had many followers. In 1914 his followers planted bombs in churches, courthouses, and police stations around New York City. Boston police thought the East Boston group might also have been behind two bombings in 1916: a church west of the city, and a police station near the inner harbor, in the North End.

In the spring of 1918, the U.S. government forced Galleani to stop publishing his newspaper. While American men were overseas fighting in the Great War, the government refused to tolerate an anarchist publication. Then in October the government passed the Anarchist Exclusion Act. Any immigrant who was not a U.S. citizen and who supported the idea of overthrowing the U.S. government would have to leave the country. Galleani was from Italy, and so were many of his followers.

Galleani and his group refused to back down. In fact, they promised more violence. They were probably the anarchists who put up the threatening posters that appeared on Boston's telephone poles in January, right before the molasses flood.

Since many of the East Boston anarchists were Italian, some Bostonians foolishly mistrusted all Italians and Italian Americans. That attitude made life harder for the many people in the North End with family roots in Italy.

As night fell, the trail of destruction left by the waves of molasses grew dark. It was harder to see the wooden wrecks that were once freight houses, offices, homes, and wagons. The sagging elevated train tracks and the giant piece of steel tank lying beneath the El looked a little less shocking in the dark. But even the blackest night could do nothing for the smell. A sour odor had replaced the fresh smell of the sea that floated across the harborside neighborhood on breezy evenings.

Who was responsible for the lost lives? Who would repay Martin and Teresa Clougherty and Mrs. O'Brien for the homes they lost? And who would repay the city of Boston for the wrecked buildings in the paving yard?

"Not us!" the owner of the molasses tank seemed to be saying. USIA's lawyer made an announcement. The company believed that "outside forces" must have caused an explosion in the tank. USIA did not explain what it meant by "outside forces," but everyone knew. The company was suggesting that anarchists had blown up the molasses tank.

Chapter 4

Who Is to Blame?

The day after the molasses flood brought big news for Boston and the nation. Nebraska had just cast the last vote needed to make the Prohibition amendment part of the Constitution. In exactly one year, it would be illegal to sell or drink alcoholic beverages anywhere in the United States.

In the meantime Martin Clougherty wanted to return to work at his bar, the Pen and Pencil. He needed to make some money before the new amendment went into effect. Many of his customers would offer him sympathy for the loss of his mother and his home. And a few would surely tease him good-naturedly about becoming

Front page of the January 16, 1919, Boston Post, *documenting the molasses disaster*

a celebrity. The headline on page seven of the *Boston Daily Globe* that day was about him: "Martin Clougherty Awoke in Sea of Sticky Molasses." But Martin was much too sore to work at the bar. His chest and legs hurt.

Martin also worried that his brother, Stephen, might be in worse shape than he was himself. His brother was thirty-two years old. But Stephen had the mind of a child, and he had almost drowned in molasses. That had to be a terrifying experience for him. As soon as Martin felt a little better, he would visit his brother at the hospital.

While Martin Clougherty rested, a giant cleanup continued in his old neighborhood. Near the damaged elevated train tracks, men were using a tall crane to remove the remains of the Cloughertys' home. When a worker heard a faint meow coming from under the wreckage, he gave a shout. The crane operator stopped the machine, and men rushed to remove some debris with their hands. They uncovered a kitten, which was in fine shape. Somehow it had managed to survive the molasses flood.

Getting rid of all the molasses was a lot harder than rescuing a kitten. Firemen hooked up their hoses to fire hydrants. For hours they aimed streams of water around the flooded neighborhood. But the water did not remove much of the molasses.

In the train yard, workers aimed water at the piles and piles of molasses-covered wreckage. Big chunks of broken wagons and trucks stuck to dented boxes of freight. It was frustrating work—and heartbreaking. Amid the debris was the body of an eighteen-year-old boy, trapped under a truck axle. The body of a man dressed in work clothes lay under the wreckage of one of the buildings in North End Park.

The cleanup seemed painfully slow to everyone. But on the third day someone had an idea. City officials ordered firemen to put a fireboat to work. From the harbor they aimed seawater at the molasses-coated sidewalks and streets.

The seawater worked. Workers were relieved to see the molasses slowly begin to disappear. The weather was cooperating, too—the

Engine 31, the Thomas A. Ring

temperature was fairly warm. As soon as it turned colder, the molasses would stiffen and become more difficult to remove.

MISSING: MONEY, POWDERED EGGS, AND A LOT OF SHORTENING

Across Commercial Street from the harbor stood a row of homes with flooded basements. Each one held at least a few feet of molasses. The molasses was covered with water, which had run off the streets and sidewalks as workers hosed them down. The fire department's master mechanic began sucking out the water and molasses with a big hydraulic siphon. The siphon slurped the water right out—but the molasses moved much more slowly.

One man who lived on Commercial Street waited anxiously for the fire department to clean out his basement. George Kakavas was a peddler who sold bananas from a small cart. First he bought great bunches of green bananas. Then he let them ripen in his basement until they turned a sunny yellow and were ready to eat.

The banana peddler knew he would have to throw out the molasses-covered bananas in his basement. But what he really wanted to find was something he had hidden between two bunches of green bananas: a box with $4,400 in it. Now he wondered whether he would ever find the box. When the police learned about the money, they placed a guard outside his home.

People stand in pools of molasses, looking at the debris. After the flood, people left their sticky footprints all over the city.

Kakavas's grown daughter, Stavroula, shared his apartment. She had stored some precious things in the basement, too, including her wedding clothing. These were gifts from her relatives in Greece. Stavroula was getting married in May.

Kakavas was not the only one who kept his savings in a box. Martin Clougherty kept all of his money in a tin box. He was luckier than Kakavas. Someone found the tin box for him while Clougherty was trying to get himself and his sister, Teresa, out of the molasses.

Martin and Teresa's mother, Bridget Clougherty, had kept her savings in a most unusual place: she wrapped it up and pinned it to her petticoat. (Women wore these thin garments underneath their dresses or skirts.) Mrs. Clougherty's package of money was fairly large. Like Kakavas the banana peddler, she had managed to save about four thousand dollars. Mrs. Clougherty knew that the Prohibition Amendment would probably become law, so she had set aside money for the family to live on when Martin's bar shut its doors. She wore her money package every day. When Mrs. Clougherty walked, the package swayed under her skirt.

While some people tried to find missing money, others looked for their horses, and still others searched for missing freight. Horace Lowell, who owned a baking supply business, lost a lot of goods on the day of the molasses flood. Before the tank burst, a truck man had come with a team of horses and a wagon to pick up a large load for Lowell and take it to one of the freight sheds in the train yard. The load included sixty pounds of powdered eggs, six pounds of cinnamon, and more than five hundred pounds of shortening.

While the truck man's team was clip-clopping down Commercial Street with his load, the molasses tank burst apart. The truck man heard a loud noise. The next thing he knew, he was on someone's doorstep. His horses and the load of baking supplies were nowhere in sight.

You can see the rivet holes in this twisted piece of metal from the molasses tank.

THE INSPECTORS ARRIVE

In the days after the molasses flood, experts arrived on the scene. They weren't looking for lost horses or cinnamon or money. And they weren't looking for the bodies of the unfortunate people who had drowned. They were all looking for answers to the same question: why did the molasses tank come apart?

Walter Wedger trudged through the molasses-filled neighborhood on the day of the flood. He dodged the water hoses, which firemen sprayed endlessly at the molasses, and tried not to disturb the rescue workers. Wedger, who worked for the Massachusetts state police, was an expert on explosives. He wanted to know whether the molasses tank had collapsed or exploded. Wedger studied the pieces of the tank that had scattered. One had hit the column supporting the elevated train with a lot of force. Another ended up at the fire station. Wedger thought there must have been an explosion. If the tank had simply collapsed, pieces of the tank would not have scattered.

But Wedger told newspaper reporters that he didn't think a bomb had made the tank explode. He knew that the molasses in the tank could ferment and produce a gas. The pressure of the gas, he concluded, had created the explosion.

Wedger knew what bomb-damaged buildings looked like. Two years earlier, he had examined a police station that was bombed just a few blocks away from the molasses tank. That blast had destroyed the police station and shattered many windows in the neighborhood. Wedger believed the anarchists had targeted the police. But he didn't think they had any reason to destroy the molasses tank.

An engineer hired by the Boston Elevated Railway Company came and examined the wreckage, too. The railway company, which operated the elevated train, wanted to know who was responsible for the tank disaster. Maybe the molasses tank was not strong enough. If that were true, the owner of the tank would owe the railway company at least $35,000. That's how much money the elevated company thought it was going to lose because of the disaster. The company would have to buy steel to fix the damaged track and columns. Steel was expensive—and it was hard to get, because the war had created a shortage.

In addition to the repair bills, the company was losing money for another reason. It would be a long time before its trains ran again between North and South stations. The company would lose all the train fares that its passengers normally would pay.

The engineer didn't agree with Walter Wedger. He thought there would have been more broken windows in the neighborhood if the tank had exploded, even if the cause of the explosion was trapped gas, and not a bomb.

The U.S. Industrial Alcohol Company, which owned the tank,

A section of the molasses tank and other debris. Men wore boots to protect their feet from the sticky goo.

also hired a number of experts to look over the disaster area. Among them were professors of chemistry at two famous local universities, Harvard University and the Massachusetts Institute of Technology. USIA hoped the professors would conclude that someone had dropped a bomb into the tank.

Three days after the flood, a distinguished man arrived on the scene. Wilfred Bolster, the chief justice of Boston's Municipal Court, waded through the molasses, which was still a couple of inches deep. Judge Bolster was going to conduct a criminal inquest. He was investigating whether a person or a company might be responsible for Mrs. Clougherty's death. If an anarchist had dropped a bomb in the molasses tank, that person could be tried in court for the death of Mrs. Clougherty. Chief Justice Bolster returned to the harborside neighborhood several times. Walter Wedger, the explosives expert, often came with him.

JUDGE BOLSTER DROPS A VERBAL BOMB

In early February Judge Bolster made his report public. Three weeks had passed since the molasses accident. Nineteen victims of the molasses flood had died.

Judge Bolster did not think there was an anarchist bomber sneaking around the molasses tank on January 15. Instead, he believed that the problem was the tank itself, which USIA had ordered to be built. It just wasn't strong enough to contain the more than two million gallons of molasses it held that day. He also agreed with Walter Wedger's analysis. The molasses probably had produced a lot of gas, which may have caused an explosion. But if the tank had been strong enough, Judge Bolster believed, it would not have exploded.

The judge thought USIA was responsible for the molasses disaster. But he didn't believe the company was the only wrongdoer. In his report he had a lot to say about another guilty party: the ordinary citizens of Boston.

"What did we do?" Bostonians probably wondered when they picked up the *Boston Daily Globe* on February 8. The headline shouted in large type, "Public Blamed for Tank Disaster in Findings of Justice Bolster."

Judge Bolster blamed Boston residents for pinching pennies. They wanted to keep their taxes low. As a result, at least one important department in the city government did not have enough money to do its job properly—the building department.

One of the building department's jobs was to study building plans and approve them. If the department thought a building or another type of structure was not going to be safe, it refused to give its approval. According to Judge Bolster, the inspectors in the building department should not have approved the plans for the molasses tank.

Judge Bolster's report went to a grand jury. This group of men also looked at the evidence gathered by police and experts, and they studied photographs. The grand jury met to decide whether USIA, the owner of the tank, had committed a crime. What crime? The construction of a weak tank, which caused people's deaths during the molasses flood.

A week after Judge Bolster issued his report, the grand jury made its decision. They did not believe USIA was guilty of a crime. The company would not be tried in a court for manslaughter (killing someone without intending to).

But USIA wasn't off the hook. The victims of the molasses flood could still sue the company with the hope of receiving money—and there were many victims. In addition to the nineteen people who died, at least forty people had been injured. A number of companies would probably sue, including the Boston Elevated Railway Company. The families of victims who died would want some money from USIA, too.

THE FLOOD SURVIVORS TRY TO RECOVER

Martin Clougherty may have been too worried about his brother, Stephen, to think about suing USIA. Stephen had been transferred from the Haymarket Relief Station to Boston City Hospital, which was larger. A few days after the flood, Martin visited Stephen for the first time. The molasses flood had changed Stephen's personality. He used to be peaceful, and now Stephen seemed terrified. He was afraid the nurses would try to poison him, or even throw him out the window. The doctors decided to transfer Stephen to a hospital for mentally ill patients.

Mrs. O'Brien had broken her jaw when she fell in the room where she was doing her wash. It was still very sore. She worried about her sister, too, who felt miserable and looked it. As Mrs. O'Brien described her later, "She had a shock, and her mouth was way around the side of her face." She may have had a stroke.

Young Antonio DiStasio had fractured his skull and stayed in the hospital. He felt sad whenever he thought about his older sister, Maria, and his friend, Pasquale, who both drowned in the flood.

John Dillon, the train car inspector, was fine. But his supervisor, who had scolded Maria for entering the train yard, died at the Haymarket Relief Station.

The cooper John Flynn developed pneumonia. He had practically flown through Number 3 freight house and landed in the icy waters of the inner harbor. Walter Merrithew, the freight clerk, had gotten caught in the same freight shed. The experience continued to give him nightmares.

The stone cutter John Barry lay in a bed in Boston City Hospital. When the firehouse caved in, a water heater and a heavy wooden beam had fallen on top of him. Now he was badly bruised and felt sore all over.

THE YANKEE DIVISION COMES HOME

Two and a half months later, on April 4, the victims of the molasses flood may have forgotten about their cares, at least for a little while. The joyful noise coming from the harbor was impossible to ignore. Antonio DiStasio could hear it from his family's new apartment in the North End on Vernon Place. George Kakavas, the banana peddler, heard it loud and clear on Commercial Street.

On that day, a big gray ship with 5,800 men from the Twenty-sixth Division of the U.S. Army landed in Boston. The ship, called the *Mount Vernon,* docked at Commonwealth Pier, about a mile and a half from Commercial Street. Although the war had ended the previous November, the men had been waiting for months to come home.

Boston gave the soldiers a hero's welcome. As the carrier approached Boston Harbor on that foggy afternoon, a parade of boats came to greet it. The lead ship, the *Monitor,* drew close to the *Mount Vernon* and "fired" donuts and chocolates at the thousands of men on the deck. A shower of sweets pelted the khaki-clad soldiers, who cheered and shouted for more. Soon the *Mount Vernon* was surrounded by every imaginable type of large and small boat, from ferries to sailboats.

Relatives of the arriving men had crammed into many of the boats. Mothers and fathers searched the smiling faces of the soldiers, who were leaning dangerously over the deck of the *Mount Vernon*. One happy man shouted, "Hello, Charlie!" An answer from the gray ship came quickly: "Hello, Dad!"

John F. Fitzgerald, Boston's ex-mayor, rode in a small power boat. As he circled the *Mount Vernon,* he sang a popular song, "Sweet Adeline," through a megaphone. When the soldiers heard his voice, they hollered, "There's Johnny Fitz!"

Thousands of people stood on the piers and on the small islands in the harbor. As soon as the crowds saw the smokestacks of the transport ship through the fog, they all cheered. Factories blew their whistles. The din continued for half an hour.

Mrs. O'Brien probably enjoyed the excitement. Maybe she even forgot about her sore jaw. She had worked hard to help raise money for these young men while they were serving their country in Europe.

ANARCHISTS COME OUT OF HIDING

By early June the mood all around the city of Boston had turned from grateful joy to anger and fear. Walter Wedger, the explosives expert, had another bomb to investigate.

On June 2 there was an explosion outside the home of Judge Albert Hayden in Newtonville, a suburb of Boston. The judge had not

Mayor John F. Fitzgerald riding in the Evacuation Day Parade

JOHN F. FITZGERALD

John F. Fitzgerald was one of the most colorful politicians in Boston's history. Bostonians fondly called him "Honey Fitz" because he was a charming man who sang with a golden voice as sweet as honey.

Fitzgerald grew up in the North End. When he was a young boy, the neighborhood was filled with Irish families like his. Hundreds of thousands of them came to the United States in the mid-1800s to escape a terrible famine in Ireland.

In winter, after a snowfall, Fitzgerald and his friends trudged up to the Boston Common to pitch snowballs at some of the richest boys in town. Boston Common was a large open area. On one side stood the state capitol building, crowned with a big gold dome. The wealthy boys lived on Beacon Hill, behind the capitol.

Fitzgerald and his friends may have been tougher. But the boys who came out of the large wooden doors near the common had an advantage. Since they lived close to the "battlefield," they could make their snowballs the night before and let them get nice and hard. Then they brought baskets filled with these icy snowballs to the common.

Honey Fitz survived the snowball fights. As a grown man he fought again with a son of one the privileged Beacon Hill families, Henry Cabot Lodge. But they fought on Capitol Hill in Washington, D.C.—and instead of snowballs, they used words.

Before he became mayor of Boston in 1906, Honey Fitz served as a representative in the U.S. Congress. He worked to defeat an anti-immigration bill proposed by Lodge, then a powerful senator.

Lodge was unhappy to see the waves of new immigrants who had been arriving in the United States in the late 1880s and 1890s. Among them were poor Italian families who poured into American cities. In Boston they settled in the North End, just like Antonio DiStasio's parents. The immigrants hoped they would have a better life. Lodge wanted to make it difficult for people like them to become citizens of the United States. His bill would require them to be able to read the U.S. Constitution in English.

When Fitzgerald objected, Lodge said angrily, "Do you think . . . Italians have any right in this country?" "As much as your father or mine," Fitzgerald shot back. (Although Congress passed the bill in 1897, President Grover Cleveland vetoed it.)

Fitzgerald believed the new immigrants would make the country richer and stronger. He never forgot his own Irish roots, and he hoped his family would continue to contribute to the country's greatness. Indeed it did: Fitzgerald's grandson John F. Kennedy (JFK) was elected president of the United States in 1960. He was only about a year and a half old when molasses flooded the harborside neighborhood in the North End where his grandfather grew up. JFK's younger brother Edward Kennedy was born thirteen years after the flood. He became one of the most skillful members of the U.S. Senate, where he served for forty-seven years.

been home, but the bomb almost killed his twenty-year-old son, and it destroyed part of the house. Red sheets of paper lay scattered around the property. On them was a message from a group calling itself the Anarchist Fighters. The anarchists promised bloody violence. "There will have to be murder," they proclaimed. "We will kill because it is necessary. . . . Long live the socialist revolution."

On that same day, bombs also went off in Washington, D.C.; Philadelphia, Pennsylvania; Paterson, New Jersey; and Cleveland, Ohio. More than half of the bombs were aimed at public officials. An anarchist organization had coordinated the attacks. The one that shocked people most that day was the bomb that exploded in Washington, D.C., outside of the home of the attorney general of the United States, Mitchell Palmer.

Fortunately, the attorney general was not killed—just the bomber. He had tripped on the attorney general's stairs. In his empty suitcase lay a red leaflet from the Anarchist Fighters. The remains of his body were scattered around the block. He was the only person killed on that terrible day. Investigators believed the bomber was Carlo Valdinoci, one of the anarchists who met together in East Boston.

Two brothers found a bloody prize—one of the bomber's feet. It was not every day that two boys came upon a lone foot. So they stored it in their refrigerator. Their poor mother discovered it and turned it in to the police.

Maybe the Anarchist Fighters had also planted a bomb in the molasses tank four and a half months earlier, on January 15. Arthur Jell thought that might be true. In fact, he hoped that it was true. Arthur Jell was an official of the U.S. Industrial Alcohol Company, which had owned the tank. Jell worried about the lawsuits that he knew were coming his way. He knew the company would have to go to court. If the company's lawyers could prove that anarchists blew up the molasses tank, then no judge or jury could claim that USIA was responsible for the molasses flood. And USIA would not have to pay any of the victims of the flood even one cent.

Chapter 5

A Flood of Stories

On August 17, 1920, John Flynn the cooper walked into the Suffolk County Courthouse, just a couple of blocks from the state capitol. More than a year and a half had passed since the day he flew through Number 3 freight house and landed in the water. Now he was finally going to tell his story in a courtroom. More than one hundred people and businesses were suing the U.S. Industrial Alcohol Company for the deaths of their family members, or damages to their own health, or the destruction of their property. Altogether they were suing USIA for one million dollars. USIA wanted all those lawsuits bundled together to save time and money, and the court agreed.

Suffolk County Courthouse, Pemberton Square

John Flynn was one of the first flood victims to come to the grand courthouse. Once inside, he climbed a flight of stairs and stood in the middle of the Great Hall. The arched ceiling soared four stories above him. Rows of carved wooden flowers and paintings filled its surface.

Surrounding Flynn near the windows of the Great Hall were sixteen life-size marble statues of men and women dressed in flowing robes, like the ancient Greeks. Each one symbolized a different word. The woman who represented Innocence wore a wreath of flowers on her head and stood beside a lamb. Guilt was a man with a long beard who crossed his hands over his chest.

Nearby stood a big bronze statue of Rufus Choate, a famous lawyer and statesman of the nineteenth century. The toe of his left shoe was very shiny because lawyers rubbed it for good luck, hoping they would win their cases. Flynn climbed more stairs and went inside a courtroom.

Hugh Ogden was acting as judge. He was not a real judge— Ogden usually worked as a lawyer. At the molasses trial he was called the auditor. Ogden was listening to all of the evidence presented by victims like John Flynn and by some engineers and other experts. Then he would write a report and suggest whether or not the case should be tried in a court with a real judge and a jury. If Ogden thought USIA was responsible for the molasses flood, he would also recommend how much money it should pay each person or company.

When Flynn looked around the courtroom, he could tell easily who the lawyers were: They all wore suits, white shirts, and ties. When his name was called, Flynn walked to the front of the room, where Hugh Ogden was sitting.

A lawyer for the plaintiffs asked Flynn what he was doing when the molasses tank collapsed. (The plaintiffs were all of the people and businesses suing USIA, including Flynn.) He replied that he was about to enter Number 3 freight house to join his friends for lunch when he heard a noise. Suddenly, Flynn explained, he felt as if a gust of wind caught him and carried him through the freight house, into the water.

"Now," the lawyer asked, "is there any object or thing that stands out in your mind that you noticed?"

"Well," Flynn replied, "I seen everything coming towards me."

"Now what do you mean 'everything'?" the lawyer wanted to know. Lawyers like details.

"Automobiles, horses and wagons, and freight cars," Flynn replied.

Next USIA's lawyer, Charles Choate, had some questions for Flynn. He was a descendant of Rufus Choate, the man who inspired the bronze statue with the shiny foot in the Great Hall. Maybe Charles Choate had rubbed his ancestor's foot for good luck so the auditor would decide that USIA was innocent. But that was not the sort of question a person asked Charles Choate. Unlike most of the other lawyers, he never seemed to smile.

"Mr. Flynn," Choate asked. "What kind of noise was this that you heard when you stepped up on the platform?"

"It sounded to me as though something was cracking and ripping," Flynn said. "And then a splash like a heavy wave that you would hear at the beach."

Choate wanted to know how high in the air Flynn thought he was.

"Probably twenty feet," Flynn said.

Choate seemed interested in the fact that Flynn had no molasses on him when he was picked up in the water by a boat.

ANTONIO DiSTASIO COMES TO COURT

About a week after Flynn's appearance in court, Antonio DiStasio arrived at the Suffolk County Courthouse with his father. He was eleven years old now. His hair hid a four-inch scar where the piece of steel from the tank had cut his head.

The enormous Great Hall probably took Antonio's breath away, and maybe his voice, too.

"What is your full name?" a lawyer for the plaintiffs asked.

"Antonio DiStasio," Antonio replied quietly.

"Now, you know, if there was a fellow on the other side of the street and you wanted him, you wouldn't talk in that tone of voice," the lawyer said. "You would holler out loud. Now, speak loudly so everybody can hear."

A court stenographer had been writing down every word that each lawyer said, and every word of each person the lawyers questioned. When Antonio opened his mouth, the person recorded what Antonio said, too. Antonio did not feel like saying much.

The lawyer asked him what he was doing when the molasses tank collapsed. Antonio said that he was playing with his sister, Maria, on Commercial Street. He didn't say that they were in the train yard near the tank. Antonio knew they were not supposed to be there.

When the lawyer was done asking questions, Charles Choate walked over to Antonio. He asked Antonio to repeat what he and Maria were doing before the molasses accident. Then he asked:

"Did Maria run into the yard where the tank was?"

"No," Antonio replied.

"Did you?"

"No," Antonio repeated.

Maybe Antonio was thinking about the statue in the Great Hall that symbolized Punishment. It was a man with a bare chest. In one hand he held a fat chain with what appeared to be a handcuff on each end. In his other hand he held an ax, which represented the worst kind of punishment.

Antonio was relieved when he could finally leave the courtroom with his father, walk past the statues in the Great Hall, and go home.

Maria DiStasio's Wood

One by one, the people who had been swept up in the powerful wave of molasses told the lawyers what had happened to them. Others who had not been injured, and so were not victims, described what they had seen.

John Dillon, the train car inspector, was questioned by a lawyer for the plaintiffs. He described Maria DiStasio gathering wood in the train yard, near the molasses tank.

The lawyer asked him to describe what he heard when the molasses tank collapsed.

"Like a lot of riveting machines working at the same time," Dillon said.

Charles Choate wanted to know more about Maria's wood.

"Are you sure she had wood in her arms?" he asked.

"I wouldn't say. I don't remember distinctly whether she had it in her arms or she had—I have a recollection that she had a piece of wood in her hand," Dillon replied.

"Which hand?" Choate wanted to know.

"I wouldn't say. I don't know." Dillon must have wondered what on earth Choate was getting at.

"Was it dark-colored?" the lawyer asked.

"I don't remember," Dillon replied. He said he thought it was about three feet long.

"How old was she?" Choate asked, referring to Maria.

Dillon guessed she was between six and eight years of age.

"Was she Italian?" Choate asked next.

"Yes," Dillon replied.

"Dark hair?"

"Yes," Dillon replied.

When Mrs. O'Brien's turn came, she described what it was like to open a door to her apartment and discover the apartment had collapsed.

"Well, I was horrified," she told a lawyer for the plaintiffs. "I closed the door again. I didn't know what to do. Then I opened it again, and a fireman put up his hand for me to stand back, you know. So I waited until the fireman came over." She was seventy-eight years old, and she was not exactly sure how her apartment and the building it was in had moved to the park and then shattered. The lawyer showed her a photo of someone being taken out of a window. "That must have been my sister," Mrs. O'Brien said.

Teresa Clougherty and Martin Clougherty told their story a few days after Mrs. O'Brien. By that time Martin was no longer operating the Pen and Pencil. Now that the Prohibition Amendment had taken effect, there wasn't much point in trying to run a bar.

Teresa described going to Martin's bedroom and telling him that something had happened to the molasses tank.

"What was the next thing you remember?" a lawyer for the plaintiffs asked.

"I don't remember anything until we were picked up."

"And where were you then?" the lawyer asked.

"Under the debris," she replied, referring to their wrecked home. Teresa also told the lawyer that their brother, Stephen, had died eleven months after the flood at a hospital for mentally ill patients.

CHARLES CHOATE GIVES USIA'S EXPLANATION OF THE FLOOD

Three weeks after the trial began, Charles Choate gave USIA's theory about why the molasses tank burst apart. He told the court, "Objects were propelled [pushed] to a considerable distance from the tank by a force independent of the molasses." And in case people in the courtroom did not catch his meaning, he added, "There will be evidence which plainly points to the action of an explosive."

Choate's earlier questions to John Dillon about Maria DiStasio had made his strategy clear. He was determined to convince Hugh Ogden that someone planted a bomb in USIA's molasses tank. And he was even willing to consider the possibility that young Maria was the bomber! Choate's argument explained why he had been interested in the gust of wind that John Flynn described pushing him through Number 3 freight house. An exploding bomb could create just that sort of wind.

The sound that the tank made as it fell apart interested the lawyers for both sides—the plaintiffs and USIA. If it sounded like an explosion, that would support Choate's argument. A ripping noise, on the other hand, might not.

Choate brought in a stream of experts who backed up his story. Many of them were engineers. A professor of engineering at the Massachusetts Institute of Technology mentioned the piece of the tank that landed near the elevated tracks. It had hit the supports of the El with a lot of force and bent one of them. If fermenting molasses had made the tank burst, and not a bomb, the professor didn't think the tank would explode with so much force.

USIA's experts even experimented with a model of the tank in Baltimore. The company collected molasses there, too. The engineers filled the model tank with molasses and put in explosives. After it burst, the damaged walls of the tank looked like those of the real tank on Commercial Street.

A Bomb Explodes on Wall Street

As the weeks rolled by in the courtroom, the lawyers must have wondered what Hugh Ogden, the auditor, was thinking. Did he find the whole idea of someone planting a bomb in the molasses tank ridiculous? If he did, the news on September 16 might have changed his mind. Someone exploded a bomb on Wall Street, near the New York Stock Exchange in New York City.

A reporter in New York City described the scene: "It was a crash out of a blue sky—an unexpected, death-dealing bolt which in a twinkling turned into shambles the busiest corner of America's financial centre and sent scurrying to places of shelter, hundreds of

New York City's financial district after a bomb exploded

wounded, dumb-stricken, white-faced men and women, fleeing from an unknown danger."

Thirty-eight people were killed. Nearby a mailman discovered some yellow sheets of paper threatening more violence. They were signed by the American Anarchists.

A Vocabulary Discussion

On September 22 one of the plaintiffs' lawyers, Endicott Saltonstall, questioned a professor of engineering at Harvard University. The professor was one of Choate's experts.

"Was this a safe tank, in your opinion, to fill with molasses, to a depth of forty-eight feet nine inches?" Saltonstall asked.

"That depends what you mean by 'safe'," the expert replied.

"What do *you* mean by 'safe'?" Saltonstall challenged him.

"I might attach different meanings to 'safe,' depending upon the circumstance," the expert replied.

"Can there be any real misunderstanding between you and myself as to what is meant by 'safe'?" Saltonstall asked in frustration.

"I think there can," the expert answered coolly.

The professor had already said in court that he thought a bomb destroyed the molasses tank. But he obviously did not want to tell Saltonstall whether the tank was safe or not. Did that mean he thought the tank was unsafe, but did not want to say so?

Hugh Ogden, the auditor, finally brought the debate about the meaning of "safe" to an end. "It seems to me . . . to call for a professor of English rather than a professor of engineering," he said.

A Tank Built in a Rush

When autumn leaves fell on the sidewalks, people were still filing in and out of Hugh Ogden's courtroom. They came and went as snow covered the courthouse steps.

In March 1921, when winter was almost over, Hugh Ogden was still in his usual seat. He had hoped the molasses hearings would be over by now. But the end was not in sight.

Damon Hall, a lawyer for the plaintiffs, decided to leave town. He wanted to ask Arthur Jell some questions, and Jell refused to come to court. He now worked for USIA in New York, and a trip to Boston was not convenient.

So Damon Hall went to New York, and Choate went along. The court stenographer went, too, and wrote down every word that was said. Later Hugh Ogden could read the stenographer's record of the conversation. The men met at the Belmont Hotel, one of the grandest in New York City.

Jell told them the early history of the molasses tank. He had asked the Hammond Iron Works company to build it in December 1914. He admitted that he wanted it built quickly.

At that time World War I was already going on in Europe. But the United States had not yet entered the war, and would not do so for another couple of years. In the meantime, the warring nations badly needed weapons and ammunition. American businesses that made either one suddenly had a lot of foreign customers. USIA was converting molasses into alcohol, which another company used to make ammunition. The sooner the huge tank was built in Boston, the more money USIA would make.

In early December 1915 the tank was still not finished. Jell urged Hammond Iron Works to get the job done quickly. He was expecting a tanker with a load of molasses to arrive in Boston on December 31. Men worked on the tank day and night and got the job done.

Jell also admitted to Hall that when the tank was finished, he skipped an important test. He did not fill the tank with water to make sure it could hold more than 2 million gallons of liquid without leaking.

"Why not?" Hall asked.

"For one reason, there was no time," Jell replied.

"Did you," Hall asked, "at any time [before] December 31, 1915, have any technical or mechanically trained man, or any steel constructionist make an examination of the tank to determine its condition?"

"I did not," Jell answered.

MANY LEAKS IN THE MOLASSES CASE

A month after his trip to New York, Damon Hall stood in Hugh Ogden's courtroom. He was ready to question one of his star witnesses.

Isaac Gonzales was called to the front of the courtroom. Gonzales was at an army training camp when the molasses flood occurred. Before joining the army, he had worked at the molasses tank for two and a half years, usually in the pump room. One of his responsibilities was to make sure the connection between the pipeline and the tank was tightly sealed when molasses was pumped into or out of the tank.

After he had been working at the tank for a while, something disturbing happened. A ship arriving from the Caribbean made a big delivery of molasses, which was pumped into the tank. The new molasses was light and warm.

"The tank had an expansion," Gonzales explained to Damon Hall, "and began to leak."

Hall asked him how big the leak was.

"Enough to make a pool, about a pail of molasses, in twenty-four hours," Gonzales replied.

"How many of those leaks were there around the tank?" Hall wanted to know.

"It started with about four and ended up with most every seam,"

Gonzales answered. He added that he spent a lot of time chasing children away from the pools.

"What did they do?" Hall asked.

"They took the molasses in cans and on sticks," Gonzales replied. If Antonio DiStasio had been in court that day, he probably would have been tempted to hide under his chair. But Antonio was in school.

Gonzales went on with his story. He said he had told Arthur Jell about the leaks. Jell sent some men to plug the leaks with caulking. But a week later the tank was leaking badly again.

And there was something else Gonzales noticed. After each new shipment of molasses arrived from the Caribbean Sea, there were about four inches of foam on the surface of the molasses in the tank. In the summer there was even more foam. Gonzales thought the molasses was fermenting. He was worried the tank might burst because of trapped gases. At least four times, Gonzales even got up in the middle of the night to open the valves in the pump room and release some of the gas (and molasses) out of the pipeline and into the inner harbor.

A BOMB THREAT

When it was Choate's turn to ask Gonzales questions, he did not ask about the leaks or the foam. He asked Gonzales about a bomb threat that Gonzales received early one spring evening in 1917.

Gonzales was on duty at the tank when the phone rang. The caller asked whether Gonzales was the superintendent of USIA. Gonzales replied that he was just a worker. The caller called him a liar. Gonzales repeated for Choate what the caller said next:

"You're a . . . liar, you are the superintendent, and we are going to blow the . . . place up!" Then the caller hung up.

Gonzales told Choate that he had reported the incident to the police. But his boss, the superintendent of the tank, thought the phone call was a joke. Choate didn't seem to think so.

The chill of early spring 1921 gave way to warmer, summery days. Hall and the other lawyers for the plaintiffs hoped they had

THE FOAM ON THE MOLASSES

Isaac Gonzales noticed foam on the surface of the molasses while it was inside the tank. The foam was created by little bubbles of carbon dioxide, which is a gas. Gonzales realized the molasses was fermenting. Tiny invisible cells in the molasses were changing the sugar in the molasses to alcohol. The cells were giving off carbon dioxide at the same time. This process is called fermentation. Some liquids will ferment in an environment where there is almost no oxygen, such as a tank. If there is enough carbon dioxide trapped in the tank, the tank can explode. USIA wanted the molasses to ferment in its factory in Cambridge, not in the molasses tank!

shown Hugh Ogden, the auditor, why the molasses tank collapsed. It obviously had problems, which Arthur Jell and some of his expert engineers were denying.

It didn't take a bomb to make a leaky tank full of molasses collapse or explode. In fact, one witness who worked for a railroad company had seen a barrel of molasses explode on a train platform. The molasses had fermented, and the barrel had no vent to let the gas out.

But Hall and the other plaintiffs' lawyers did not know whether Hugh Ogden agreed with them. After all, everyone knew there were anarchists in Boston. And the anarchists were more than willing to plant a bomb where it would do a lot of damage. One of them had even made a threatening phone call to USIA, which Gonzales answered. The molasses flood had certainly caused terrible destruction. Mrs. O'Brien, Stephen Clougherty, young Antonio DiStasio, and many other victims of the flood had experienced it personally.

Chapter 6

A Real or Mythical Bomber?

In March 1922 John Flynn, the cooper, entered the Great Hall of the courthouse one more time. More than a year and a half had passed since the first time he had answered the lawyers' questions in the courtroom. Now the auditor, Hugh Ogden, wanted to hear about his aches and pains. If Ogden decided that the U.S. Industrial Alcohol Company was responsible for the molasses flood, he would have a lot more work to do. He would have to suggest how much money USIA should pay each business that was harmed, each living victim, and each dead victim's family.

Flynn repeated his story about how he landed in the icy water behind Number 3 freight house. He described his terrible headache, too.

"Anything else?" a lawyer for the plaintiffs asked.

"Yes. I couldn't breathe," Flynn replied. "I had a wicked pain in my left side."

One of USIA's lawyers asked Flynn about an unusual accident he had after the flood. Flynn was at Braves Field watching the reenactment of a battle from the Great War. The soldiers were actors, but they had real weapons.

"I was looking at the performance," Flynn explained, "and I got struck with some kind of missile from the explosives they were using there."

Hugh Ogden, the auditor, was very interested. He had fought in France during the Great War. "Oh, yes. I remember it," he said about the performance. He could not resist teasing Flynn a little. "You fared worse at Braves Field than I did on the battle line. I got by all right."

Flynn, on the other hand, suffered from a punctured eyelid. USIA wanted to make it clear that they would owe him no money for that problem.

Teresa Clougherty came to court a month later. She had not gotten over the loss of her mother, her brother Stephen, and her home. Before the molasses flood she had enjoyed going to parties and to the theater. Now, at age twenty-six, she told a plaintiffs' lawyer that she no longer wanted to be with crowds of people.

The stonecutter, John Barry, was probably worse off than anyone else who had been injured by the flood and lived to tell the tale. He wasn't strong enough to cut stone anymore. When the firehouse collapsed, the weight of a heater and some heavy wooden timbers injured his back and left knee. "He has aged," his doctor told one of the plaintiffs' lawyers.

Hugh Ogden listened carefully to everyone's story. He listened to the doctors who described the medical problems of the flood's victims. But his attention may have wandered a little when the engineers returned to the courtroom. They seemed to go over every rivet hole and seam that remained of the molasses tank. If Ogden daydreamed for a moment or two, no harm was done. The court stenographer was hard at work, writing down every word that was said.

CHOATE MAKES HIS CLOSING ARGUMENT

In the fall of 1923 the lawyers were ready to make their closing arguments. The hearings had gone on for more than three years. The lawyers had called more than three thousand witnesses. Before Hugh Ogden reached a decision on the case, he planned to read the written transcript of what was said in court. It was about twenty-five thousand pages long!

Charles Choate, USIA's leading lawyer, went first. He pointed out that before the molasses tank burst on January 15, 1919, it was holding 2,319,000 gallons of molasses. In August 1918 the tank had been filled with even more molasses. At that time, it held 2,379,000 gallons, Choate said. Yet it did not burst. "If the tank . . . did not have sufficient structural strength to withstand a load of molasses which was in at the time of the disaster, it would have failed the first time it was filled with a similar load," Choate argued.

Choate declared that the tank was built by experienced builders. He said the builders made the tank with "first-class quality steel."

According to Choate, someone had planted explosives in the tank. It was the most logical explanation for the molasses flood. He reminded Hugh Ogden that a police station had been bombed just a few blocks from the tank. A few years later the home of a Boston judge was bombed. And didn't Isaac Gonzales receive a bomb threat when he was on duty at the tank? In fact, someone actually *did* find a bomb in another molasses tank owned by USIA, in Brooklyn, New York. Fortunately, that one did not explode.

DAMON HALL POKES HOLES IN CHOATE'S ARGUMENT

If one or two people had fallen asleep during the unsmiling Choate's closing arguments, then Damon Hall woke them up. Hall made fun of Choate's "mythical anarchist, climbing at high noon up the side of a fifty-foot tank, in the heart of a busy city, with hundreds of people about." How, Hall wondered out loud, could this mythical bomber have managed to drop a bomb in the tank and escape through the railroad yard where people were working? How did he or she simply "disappear . . . into thin air"?

According to Hall, Choate's attempt to prove there was a bomber showed how desperate he was. "He even seizes upon a little child, a little girl, as being possibly the author of this outrage [the molasses flood]," Hall exclaimed. He was referring to Choate's questions for John Dillon about the wood in Maria DiStasio's hands.

Hall turned his attention to the rush of air that the cooper John Flynn believed had pushed him through Number 3 freight house and into the water. "It wasn't any rush of air which carried Flynn through the freight house wall," Hall argued. He said that Flynn ran when he saw danger, just like everyone else. "My feeling is that Flynn ran the same as if a can had been tied to the tail of [a] dog," Hall said.

Hugh Ogden had a question for Hall. If Flynn was running from the molasses, which was already in the freight shed, why didn't he have any molasses on him when he was picked up later in the water?

Hall had a ready explanation. "Well, it is somewhere in the case, if your Honor please . . . that the only way they found of effectually getting rid of the molasses down there was by pumping up salt sea water . . . and my theory has always been that if he did get any spatters of molasses on him or did get into the molasses, that very likely the action of the salt water took out the molasses."

Now Hall was ready to present his own explanation for why the molasses tank burst. He reminded Ogden that Choate had painted a dark picture. In Choate's picture the anarchists lurking in Boston had been plotting to destroy the molasses tank.

But Hall didn't think the anarchists had any reason to destroy the tank. He had a different theory. "Well, now, if your honor please," Hall said. "I am going to paint a [picture] which . . . doesn't necessitate the belief in ghosts and ghostly bombs and all that sort of thing."

According to Hall, the U.S. Industrial Alcohol Company was in too much of a hurry. "The first rush of the war was on," he said. "The opportunity was open to American [businesses] to make big money." They were in such a rush that they did some very dangerous things, Hall explained. They built a tank that was going to hold millions of gallons of liquid. And where did they put it? Right in the middle of a busy city neighborhood—near a playground, for heaven's sake.

And to make things worse, Hall said, USIA asked Arthur Jell to supervise the construction of the tank. Jell didn't have the right experience for the job. He knew how to manage money, not construction. The result was a tank that wasn't strong enough. It leaked.

HEARING CLOSED

On September 29, 1923, Hugh Ogden declared that the hearings for the molasses case were closed. He made it clear that he would need many months to read over the thousands of pages of testimony before he reached his decision.

Of course, the plaintiffs hoped Ogden would decide the U.S. Industrial Alcohol Company owed them money. But in the meantime, they went on with their lives.

Martin Clougherty closed down his new hotel near the ocean before the arrival of another cold New England winter. Walter Merrithew, who had experienced such terrible nightmares after the flood, now played sports and went dancing when he had free time.

George Kakavas, the banana peddler, had returned to Greece, where he died. His daughter, Stavroula, cooked and kept house for herself and her new husband.

Antonio DiStasio was just beginning a new year of school in the North End. John Barry, who had been a stonecutter, now did office work to support his twelve children.

John Flynn had become famous around Boston. People were amazed by his story of riding through the freight house on a gust of wind and plunging into the icy waters of the inner harbor. But his moment of fame was over now. He went on with his work handling freight and fixing barrels at his new job on a wharf in the North End.

CASE DECIDED

In late April 1925 Hugh Ogden reached a decision. More than six years had passed since a wave of molasses, taller and more powerful than the waves at the beach, had turned a small harborside neighborhood upside down. And more than a year and a half had passed since Ogden declared the hearings were over.

In his long and carefully written report, Ogden reviewed some of the evidence he had heard during three long years of hearings, and he explained how he reached his decision.

USIA's lawyers had argued that the deep, rumbling sound heard by some witnesses proved there was an explosion. "Whether a sound resembles thunder, or the fall of a load of boards, or the crushing of a peach basket obviously depends to a large degree upon the power of the individual to hear clearly and report accurately," Ogden wrote. So he ignored that evidence.

USIA had reminded the court that there were people in Boston, anarchists, who committed evil, destructive acts. But no one had seen a bomber, Ogden pointed out. And no one had found any remains from a bomb.

Ogden admitted that he felt he could drown in the flood of technical evidence given by USIA's many experts, and the plaintiffs' experts, too. Speaking of himself, he said, "The auditor has at times felt that the only rock to which he could safely cling was the obvious fact that at least one-half the scientists must be wrong."

In the end, though, Ogden had no doubts about where the blame lay. In his report, he pointed a steady finger in one direction—at USIA. They had rushed to build a tank in the middle of a large city. Before filling it with molasses, they didn't thoroughly test its strength or get an expert to inspect it. And when the tank began leaking, they mostly ignored the leaks, which had worried several witnesses. The company should have taken better care of the tank, Ogden wrote, "because of the appalling [shocking] possibility of damage." According to Hugh Ogden's calculations, USIA owed the plaintiffs about $300,000 all together.

USIA Pays the Plaintiffs

Ogden's decision was great news for the plaintiffs and their lawyers, including Damon Hall. But Hall thought USIA should pay more. So he demanded another trial, this time with a jury. USIA, and its leading lawyer, Charles Choate, did not think they could win another trial. They offered to pay more money, and the two sides reached a deal.

The lawyers, the plaintiffs, and USIA kept some of the details of their agreement a secret. According to the *Boston Daily Globe,* the company agreed to pay between $500,000 and $1,000,000. It paid a family like Antonio DiStasio's, who had lost a loved one in the flood, about $7,000. (That's about $87,000 in 2010 dollars.) People who were injured received less. John Barry, for example, received $4,000 (worth $50,000 in 2010). The Boston Elevated Railway Company collected $115,000 (about $1,435,000 in 2010) for the damage caused to its tracks.

THE MOLASSES FLOOD MAKES A DIFFERENCE

Twenty-one people died because of the molasses flood, including two children: Maria DiStasio and Pasquale Iantosca. It's hard to imagine anything good coming of such a tragedy. But people do learn from big mistakes.

Just a couple weeks after the molasses flood, Chief Justice Wilfred Bolster had made people angry. He declared the Boston Building Department needed to do its job better. (He also said Boston residents needed to pay higher taxes to support the department's work.)

The building department was listening. It demanded that designers of buildings and other large structures give the department more information before the department would give out a building permit. The department realized that if someone had taken a closer look at the plans for the molasses tank, he or she might have noticed that it should have been designed to be much stronger. Massachusetts was not the only state to learn from the disaster. Other states that had been giving out building permits freely tightened up their regulations, too.

The victims who survived the molasses flood never forgot it. But the disaster eventually faded from the memories of most Bostonians. For years, though, a reminder lingered in the neighborhood where the tank once sat. It was the smell of molasses. On hot days, it sometimes drifted all the way to the state house.

By 1995 the smell had faded. Maybe that's why Boston's historical society decided it was time to place a more permanent reminder in the harborside neighborhood. Workers nailed a historic plaque to a stone wall outside of a park. In the park, kids play baseball and grownups play bocce where John Flynn once fixed barrels in the train yard and where Antonio DiStasio and his sister and friends licked molasses from a leaky tank.

Boston Molasses Flood

On January 15, 1919, a molasses tank at 529 Commercial Street exploded under pressure, killing 21 people. A 40-foot wave of molasses buckled the elevated railroad tracks, crushed buildings and inundated the neighborhood. Structural defects in the tank combined with unseasonably warm temperatures contributed to the disaster.

THE BOSTONIAN SOCIETY

Commemorative plaque on Commercial Street

Acknowledgments

My first thank-you goes to my husband, John, a loving and generous partner and my first reader, always. He has helped in countless other ways, especially when a deadline neared. I thank my sister, Cecile, who gave the manuscript a 10 at a crucial moment, when it was still a tender work-in-progress. And my son, Noah, for sharing my enthusiasm for well-chosen words and well-made cookies.

Many thanks go to the members of my critique group in Concord, Massachusetts, led by Joannie Duris, for their sharp observations and those encouraging words in the margins; and to my friend Anne Mackin for her terrific feedback and writerly support.

I appreciate the help of my editor, Emily Mitchell, who read the manuscript with so much care and intelligence and offered many great suggestions for making it better. Thanks to Diane Earley for producing such a handsome book, and to Sarah Brannen for making the beautiful map. And I feel very lucky to have such a fine agent, Stephen Fraser, in my corner.

Stephen Puleo's fine account of the molasses flood, *Dark Tide,* pointed me toward two invaluable sources: The transcript of the molasses flood hearings, *Dorr v. U.S. Industrial Alcohol,* is housed at the Social Law Library, in the John Adams Courthouse, the very building where the hearings took place. My thanks to Brian Harkins, Esq., reference librarian, and to June Strojny, director of library operations, for permission to read the transcript and for help in getting all forty volumes to the reading room. More thanks go to Elizabeth Bouvier, the head of archives at the Supreme Judicial Court Archives, for her help in securing the second source, Hugh Ogden's *Auditor's Report* to the Superior Court.

Photo Credits

Front Matter
Cover, courtesy of the Boston Public Library, Print Department. Page i, courtesy of the Bostonian Society/Old State House Museum. Page ii, courtesy of the Bostonian Society/ Old State House Museum. Page v, Library of Congress. Page vi, Library of Congress. Page viii, Library of Congress.

Chapter 1
Page 1, Library of Congress. Page 3, courtesy of the Bostonian Society/Old State House Museum. Page 4, Library of Congress. Page 5, Library of Congress. Page 6, courtesy of the Bostonian Society/Old State House Museum. Page 10, Library of Congress.

Chapter 2
Page 13, Library of Congress. Page 16, courtesy of the Boston Public Library, Leslie Jones Collection. Page 22, courtesy of the Boston Public Library, Leslie Jones Collection.

Chapter 3
Page 25, Library of Congress. Page 26, Library of Congress. Page 32, courtesy of the Boston Public Library, Leslie Jones Collection. Page 36, courtesy of the Boston Public Library, Leslie Jones Collection. Page 39, courtesy of the Boston Public Library, Leslie Jones Collection. Page 40, courtesy of the Bostonian Society/Old State House Museum. Page 42, Library of Congress. Page 43, Library of Congress.

Chapter 4
Page 45, Library of Congress. Page 46, courtesy of the Boston Public Library, Newspaper Archive. Page 48, courtesy of Frank Fitzgerald and the Boston Sparks Association. Page 50, courtesy of the Bostonian Society/Old State House Museum. Page 53, courtesy of the Bostonian Society/Old State House Museum. Page 56, courtesy of the Boston Public Library, Leslie Jones Collection. Page 64, courtesy of the Boston Public Library, Print Department. Page 65, Library of Congress. Page 66, Library of Congress.

Chapter 5
Page 69, Library of Congress. Page 70, courtesy of the Boston Public Library, Print Department. Page 79, Library of Congress. Page 85, courtesy of the Bostonian Society/Old State House Museum.

Chapter 6
Page 87, Library of Congress. Page 98, courtesy of Nick Poulos.

Index